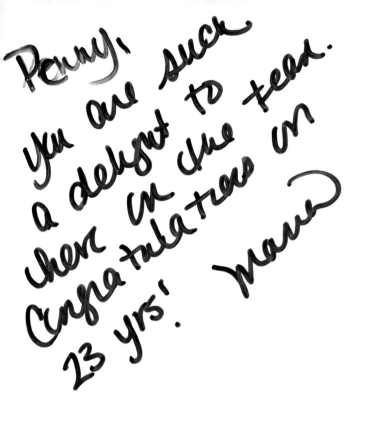

Penny,
You are such
a delight to
them on the team.
Congratulations on
23 yrs!. Maria

The Key

CELEBRATED PEOPLE
UNLOCK
THEIR SECRETS TO LIFE

LINDA SOLOMON

STEWART, TABORI & CHANG ✦ NEW YORK

Published in 2007 by Stewart, Tabori & Chang
An imprint of Harry N. Abrams, Inc.

Library of Congress Cataloging-in-Publication Data:

Solomon, Linda (Linda Rappaport)

  The key : celebrated people unlock their secrets to life / Linda Solomon.

    p. cm.

  ISBN 978-1-58479-630-5

   1. Success. 2. Conduct of life. 3. Americans—Quotations. 4. Locks and
keys—Miscellanea. I. Title.

BJ1611.2.S65 2007

170'.44—dc22   2007013423

Editor: Jennifer Levesque
Designer: Anna Christian
Production Manager: Jacquie Poirier

The text of this book was composed in Mrs Eaves.

Printed and bound in China

10 9 8 7 6 5 4 3 2 1

HNA
harry n. abrams, inc.
a subsidiary of La Martinière Groupe
115 West 18th Street
New York, NY 10011
www.hnabooks.com

A smile is the key that fits
the lock of everybody's heart.

Anthony J. D'Angelo
THE COLLEGE BLUEBOOK

This book is dedicated to
my husband, Barry Solomon, and my mother, Mona Rappaport.
Their love has provided every important key.

In memory of my father, Daniel J. Rappaport,
whose key words of wisdom will always remain with me.

Live, Love, Laugh

✦ Introduction ✦

I have always saved keys. A small brass key to unlock my five-year diary, a sturdy key to my first car, and an exquisite silver key and key ring to bungalow 6B, our honeymoon cottage at the Beverly Hills Hotel. Keys to open new doors in one's life.

When I started working on this book I asked my mother, a saver of everything, if she saved keys. She handed me two bags. One was a blue velvet pouch filled with wonderful cabinet and clock keys that belonged to my grandmother. I was amazed by the beauty and unique style of each vintage key.

The other bag belonged to my sister Jill. It was filled with colorful hotel keys and key rings from our family vacations. One of Jill's keepsakes was a key engraved with the words "Tucson Key" attached to a key ring from the El Dorado Lodge, a wonderful place that closed years ago. Keys have a history. Just like photographs, they bring back memories.

I then began a photographic journey to find the "right" key. I have always believed photography teaches us to not just look, but really see. The words engraved on keys communicate certain qualities. The key is a metaphor and, if matched with the right person, each key has a soul.

Throughout my career as a photojournalist, I have photographed and interviewed famous people. I selected people for this book who are synonymous with special qualities. I have asked these remarkable people to share their insights and their key words of wisdom. They have also shared another quality—compassion—since their words will benefit breast cancer research.

I hope the photographs of each key provide a *different* way to see the real person by opening our eyes to their words.

The words are honest, often surprising, and always enlightening. "Once you find your soulmate (it may take a few tries), don't ever take it for granted," says Aerosmith's Joe Perry. "Always try to find the magic in life," the legendary actor Jack Lemmon taught his oldest son, Chris. And what's the key to asking the right question? "Listen to what's been said before," says broadcast journalist Barbara Walters.

Life has secrets that, ultimately, are best when shared. So come, turn the page, turn the key, and unlock the wisdom within.

Linda Solomon

· The Keys ·

The Key to Winning

You get out of it what you put into it.
If you don't put any effort into it,
you won't get the results,
but more importantly,
you don't deserve them.

Tiger Woods
ATHLETE

The Key to a Timeless Look

No overhead lighting!

Christie Brinkley
MODEL AND ACTRESS

The Key to a Lasting Career

Having two creative disciplines that I have followed all my life:
singing and painting. When I perform, I interact with
my musicians and the audience; it is a very social endeavor.
When I paint, it is just myself and a blank canvas, that's it.
Singing and painting create a yin/yang balance because they
complement each other. I am able to always be in a creative zone,
but never have to feel burned out by doing just one thing.

Tony Bennett
SINGER AND ARTIST

"Tony" Bennett   Benedetto

ATLANTIC

45 R.P.M.

OS 13061

Pub., East-Time-
Walco, BMI
Time: 2:26

VOCAL
A-11704 SP
FROM
ATLANTIC
2403

RESPECT
(Otis Redding)
ARETHA FRANKLIN

The Key to Respect

Acknowledging that the world does not revolve around you alone.

Aretha Franklin
SINGER

The Key to Staying on Top

Stay on top of everything.

Take nothing for granted; don't lose momentum;

work today as if it were the first day on the job.

Stay in tune and up to date with everything

and everybody and all the trends.

Keep your talent and wit sharpened, and

never count your money before you count your blessings.

Dolly Parton
SINGER AND ACTRESS

The Key to Staying Grounded

Our home chores were the thing that always kept it real for us.

We had to help with dinner chores every night,

keep our rooms neat, and take care of our pets.

We also were taught to share and to volunteer our time from an early age.

Sometimes I can remember not being happy about it,

but now I am so grateful to my parents for teaching me respect,

to be humble, and how to be a good family member.

Hilary Duff
ACTRESS AND SINGER

The Key to Growth

A ship is always safe in the harbor . . .
but that's not what ships are built for—
challenges are what ultimately measure
your fortitude and character.

Katie Couric
BROADCAST JOURNALIST

The Key to a Legacy

. . . is to leave one.

My legacy is made manifest in my children,

just as I carry my father's legacy

and he carried his father's, and so on.

If my children merely echo me,

then I have failed.

My purpose in life—my legacy—is to

lift them to the next level.

Edsel Ford II
FORD MOTOR COMPANY
GREAT-GRANDSON OF HENRY FORD

The Key to Character

I have come to understand the purest,
deepest meaning of character.
In those human beings I know,
character is more than a word.
It is more than an element independently
floating high above us, waiting for someone,
or something, to elevate itself within
range of its touch. In those people I know,
character is not a condition called into
existence by words imaginatively arranged.

It is not a compliment—nor a distraction
ceremoniously bestowed by the state.
In those people I know, it is an
accompaniment. It never comes out of thin
air; it always travels in close company with
other forces. It is almost always found side
by side with integrity—or shoulder
to shoulder with decency. Step by step
it moves alongside fidelity, honesty,
selflessness, and compassion.

It is always there to heal when dignity is
stripped from human life and trampled
on with calculated disregard. Character,
like hope, dreams, and expectations, is a
driving force in human beings that prepares
the way for the emergence of the best of all
there is inside us.

Sidney Poitier
ACTOR

The Key to Equality

. . . is empathy, which is why it is the most revolutionary of all emotions. Societies that try to divide people by sex or race or class or ethnicity or sexuality—they all do their best to break the natural leap of empathy from one human being to another, especially when we are young and our brains are still malleable.

Empathy can be broken by social pressure—humans are communal creatures—but it's also true that this gift of empathy is part of our evolutionary equipment; it helps us to survive as a species. Our saving grace on this Spaceship Earth will come not so much from learning equality as from unlearning inequality.

Gloria Steinem
AUTHOR AND ACTIVIST

The Key to Believing in Oneself

Everybody should.

It comes from my parents, who had a lot of confidence in me

and instilled in me the sense that if I worked hard I could achieve,

and if I believed in something I should stick with it.

The other thing my parents gave me is my faith.

If you see yourself, and I was raised to see myself, as part of a divine creation,

you have a responsibility to make the world better. It's a real motivator.

If you feel that your existence here is no accident,

it helps you believe in yourself even if you fail, as you sometimes will.

Last year I lost the Democratic primary; I picked myself up and said

I am going to run as an independent, and that worked out.

Senator Joseph Lieberman
UNITED STATES SENATOR

The Key to Strength

Clarity of purpose.
Clarity of purpose gives you the mental
and physical strength to achieve your goal.

Martina Navratilova
ATHLETE

The Key to Obtaining the Brass Ring

One pathway to success—utilized by me and my four siblings—is to pick parents who already own a successful business! If that's not an option, then take to heart the phrase "thinking outside the box." My Scottish grandfather, B. C. Forbes, who founded our company, came to America more than a hundred years ago. He was one of ten children and possessed little money and only a grade-school education. When he hit these shores, he was repeatedly turned down by editors to be a business reporter.

Finally he went to an editor and offered to work for free,
saying he trusted that the man would have the integrity
to hire him if he demonstrated his worth to the
newspaper. My grandfather finally got his first job
that way. Still brimming with energy, he subsequently
obtained, using a nom de plume, a second job with
another publication. One of the proudest moments
in his life came when the two editors got into an argument
as to who had the best business reporter—in both cases,
it was my grandfather.

Another example: One day as a reporter, B. C. Forbes,
a tight-fisted Scotsman, stunned his friends when
he bought two fancy suits and rented a room at the
Waldorf Hotel, then indisputably the finest in the nation.
Had he taken leave of his senses? His friends worried.
No—in those days, major shakers of industry and finance
congregated at the Waldorf at the end of the work day.
My grandfather felt if he was properly dressed and a
resident, these worthies would see him in a different light
than as simply a grubby reporter, and thus he could get
information and insights from these personalities that
he could never obtain otherwise. The gamble paid off.
Vision. Courage. Persistence. An ability to pick oneself up after a
setback. These are essential for true success.

Steve Forbes
EDITOR AND CEO

The Key to
a Lasting First Impression

Concentrate on the other person,
thus downplaying yourself, and in so doing,
you will come across as a compassionate
human being, with the blessed capacity
of thinking out and beyond yourself.

Letitia Baldrige
AUTHOR, CHIEF OF STAFF TO FORMER FIRST LADY JACQUELINE KENNEDY

The Key to Team Leadership

✦ Allowing your players to have their own identity,
   but within the parameters of the total team concept.

✦ Getting your players to maximize their ability by challenging them
   to perform to their utmost ability.

✦ Instill the confidence to be able to concentrate and relax
   at the same time, in the biggest situations.

✦ Create an environment that your players best survive in.

✦ Getting your players to perform like they're in first place,
   but prepare like they're in second place.

✦ Don't ask your team to win, but ask them to prepare to win.

Jim Leyland
MANAGER, DETROIT TIGERS

The Key to Sophistication

. . . is knowledge translated as naturalness.
It is a total lack of pretense.

Carolina Herrera
DESIGNER AND CEO

The Key to Putting Your Best Face Forward

A great pair of sunglasses and a smile.

But seriously, it's about how you see the world—

choosing to trust it and the people in it.

We've all experienced disappointments in our lives,

but what I learned from my mother is to

expect the best out of people and situations and

you will have a better chance of getting it.

If all else fails, smile—and don't forget your shades!

Cindy Crawford
MODEL AND ACTRESS

The Key to Being
the Perfect Apprentice

Be a team player while knowing

how to operate effectively as a leader.

It's a fine balance, and it's a quality that is absolutely necessary.

Later on, these apprentices will find that knowing

how to be both will help them in business negotiations

as well as many of the places life will bring them.

It's a life skill worth acquiring.

Donald J. Trump
ENTREPRENEUR AND CEO

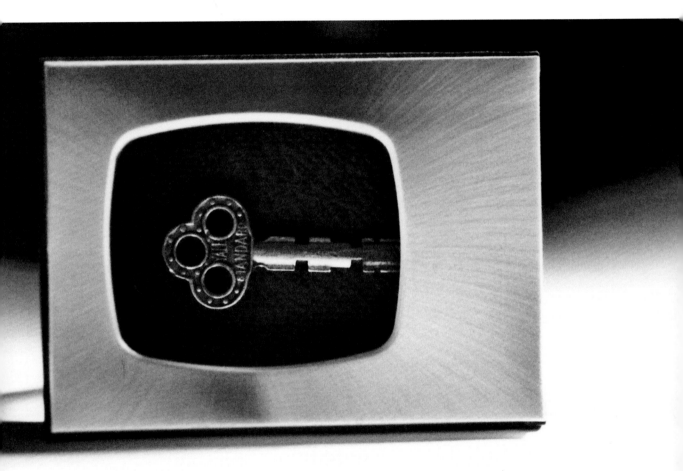

The Key to Making Someone Feel Special

. . . is to see and value them for who they are and not what you wish them to be.

Ann Curry
BROADCAST JOURNALIST

The Key to Being Cool

Not needing a key.

Samuel L. Jackson
ACTOR

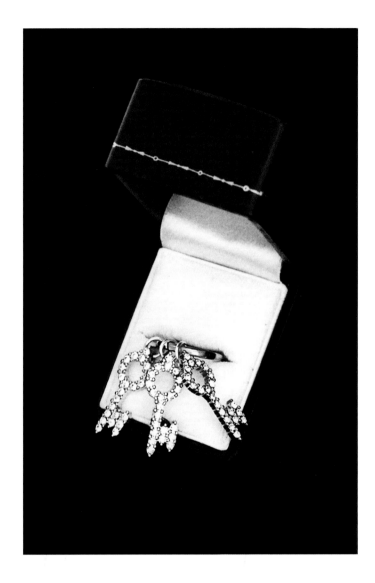

The Key to
a Successful Marriage

You need a ring of keys:

God ✦ Truth and Honesty ✦ Forgiveness ✦ Courage ✦ Joy
✦ Laughter ✦ Wisdom ✦ Strength ✦ Imagination ✦ Respect ✦
Tolerance ✦ Charity ✦ Good Food ✦ Friendship
✦ That Thing Which Has No Name

LaTanya Richardson Jackson
ACTRESS, WIFE OF ACTOR SAMUEL L. JACKSON

The Key to Being First

Being willing to take a risk.

In the movie *Chariots of Fire*,

a runner turned to his wife and said,

"If I can't win, I won't run,"

to which she responded,

"If you don't run, you can't win."

That applies to most of life's challenges.

Geraldine A. Ferraro

FIRST FEMALE VICE PRESIDENTIAL CANDIDATE
AND FORMER UNITED STATES CONGRESSWOMAN

The Key to Self-Reliance

Knowing who you are and honoring
and loving and trusting that person.

Olivia Newton-John
SINGER AND ACTRESS

The Key to Hope

Knowing that fear is just a lack of imagination.

Melissa Etheridge

SINGER

The Key to Unlocking a Fear

Because fears are born within,
confronting them, believing in your ability
to prevail, and acting on that belief
is the ultimate key to freedom.

Dr. Phil
PSYCHOLOGIST AND TALK SHOW HOST

The Key to Always Believing the Cup Is Half Full

Making sure the cup is filled with your favorite wine.

Seriously, I've always thought the cup

should never be completely full,

because then there's no room left for growth.

Meredith Vieira

BROADCAST JOURNALIST

The Key to
Finding a Soulmate

. . . involves analysis,

and I never mix analysis with romance

or soul-matedness,

or whatever it may be called.

Attempts to define or

summarize such matters

are doomed from the start.

Robert James Waller
AUTHOR, *THE BRIDGES OF MADISON COUNTY*

The Key to Beauty

Feeling good in your own skin.
Letting a healthy lust for life
shine from the inside out.

Kim Novak
ACTRESS AND ARTIST

The Key to Making Music

Respond to the world around you.

Be like a sponge.

Fortunately, I can then express those feelings

in my music.

Burt Bacharach

COMPOSER

The Key to
Getting a Great Score

Having a burning desire to do so,
and a willingness to work hard at your game.
Golf is a lifelong joy to play
when you find out how easy it can actually be.

Arnold Palmer
ATHLETE

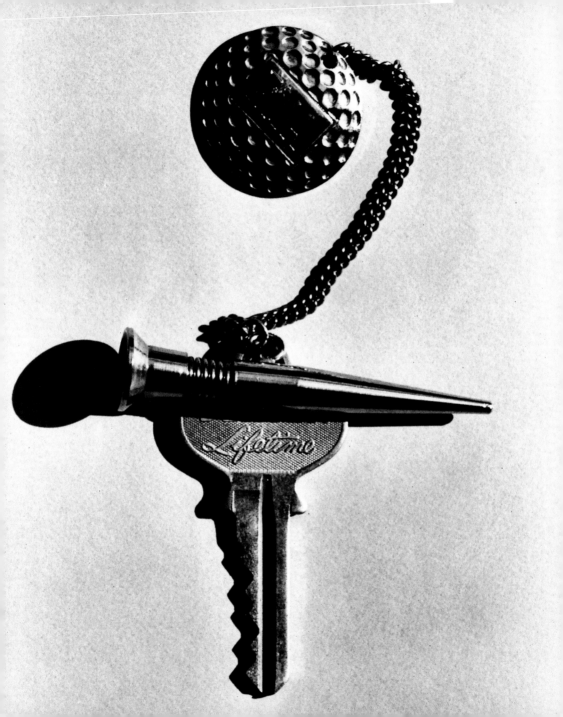

The Key to Friendship

Loyalty, laughter, support . . .
and the key to use your country house!

Jill Rappaport
ENTERTAINMENT JOURNALIST

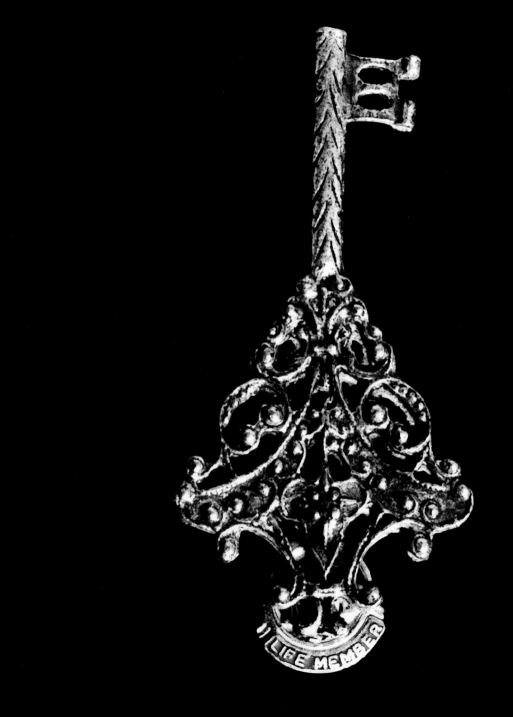

The Key to
Living Life to the Fullest

Achieving and maintaining optimum health.
If you've got that, you can accomplish anything.

Dr. Andrew Weil
PHYSICIAN AND AUTHOR

The Key to
Achieving a Career Goal

If you're pursuing what you
are meant to be doing,
you don't say "if," you say "how?"

John Lloyd Young
TONY AWARD WINNER, *JERSEY BOYS*

The Key to Negotiation

Preparation. Everything hinges on that.

I learned many lessons from my father, James R. Hoffa.

Many of those lessons were about negotiating,

one of the cornerstones of a good labor union.

He was one of the toughest negotiators to ever sit at a

bargaining table. Every day, the Teamsters Union is

negotiating in one way or another. Whether it's in the

halls of Congress or an arbitration with management,

we're always negotiating. Mostly, though, it is with

contracts between our members and their employers.

In any case, preparation is the key. When I say preparation,

though, I'm talking about many different things.

Preparation to determine your priorities in negotiations.

Preparation in knowing who will be sitting across the table from you in negotiations. Preparation to determine how much you can ask for and how much you can give. Preparation, though, isn't the only thing—just the most important. In negotiation, being flexible is paramount. Give yourself and the people you're negotiating with room to compromise. You can't take an "all or nothing" approach. My father always stressed that when negotiating, you need to be tough but fair. Make sure you give the person on the other side of the table a way to accept your proposal without looking weak. He reminded me that embarrassing your counterpart could always come back and bite you in the rear in future negotiations.

Also, be honest. In negotiation, neither side is going
to tell their strategy to everyone, but being honest
is important. Don't play "gotcha." Your word
should be good. When the Teamsters Union negotiates
contracts, those contracts are continuing agreements.
If you're not honest, it's going to come back to haunt you.
It's good to be tough, but much better to be honorable.

James P. Hoffa, Jr.
PRESIDENT OF THE INTERNATIONAL BROTHERHOOD OF TEAMSTERS

The Key to
a Signature Style

Come to terms with who you are and enjoy it!
Put your own individual spin on fashion
and be confident!

Diane von Furstenberg
DESIGNER AND CEO

The Key to Self-Expression

A commitment to trusting and developing ideas with daring perseverance.

LeRoy Neiman
ARTIST

The Key to Design

Creating a strong statement

that evokes an emotional response.

Edward T. Welburn, Jr.
VICE PRESIDENT, GLOBAL DESIGN, GENERAL MOTORS CORPORATION

The Key to Courage

. . . is positive thinking.

Champion athletes don't go into a competition thinking,
"I hope I don't lose." They think, "I'm going out there
to win this." You just have to take that first step . . . then
the next one . . . and then the next one. We all have to
face things in life that are just terrible, but sometimes you
find courage when you least expect it. You are forced in
a direction you never would have picked, but you move
forward. I promise that you'll find you can do things you
never thought you had the strength for.

Peggy Fleming
OLYMPIC FIGURE SKATER

The Key to
Asking the Right Question

Listen to what's been said before.

Barbara Walters
BROADCAST JOURNALIST

The Key to Introspection

Don't spend too long in there;
you'll never get out!

Kelsey Grammer
ACTOR

The Key to
Changing Your Life

For me, the key to changing my life
has been in finding fulfillment
and meaning in service to others and
making a difference in people's lives.

Enid Zuckerman
FOUNDER OF CANYON RANCH

The Key to Creating a Brand

There are two important underpinnings. Number one is truth.
All great brands, whether they are products, people, or services,
start with truth. You can't fake it. Stay true to your core set of values.
The second is consistency. One of the great examples of brand
or image is Madonna. Although she has evolved through the years,
it is always cutting-edge sexuality. She came on the scene
in the eighties with *Like a Virgin*; now in her forties, she's a sexy mom
horseback riding. She's never strayed from what she's about . . .
once again, it's truth and consistency.

Donny Deutsch
ADVERTISING EXECUTIVE AND TALK SHOW HOST

The Key to Stardom

An Academy Award winner told me
when you represent young actresses,
if they handle themselves
with dignity and safety,
they can be in the business
as long as they want.

Norman Brokaw
CHAIRMAN OF THE BOARD, WILLIAM MORRIS AGENCY

The Key Advice
I Learned from My Dad

Always try to find the magic in life.

In so many words his father said that to him, and in his own way
he said it to me: As far as anyone knows, before every take of
every film or any performance Jack Lemmon ever did, he would
say the words, "magic time." Anyone who has ever seen those
performances knows the man was good to his word. But even
though he showed millions the world over that magic on the silver
screen, I was blessed to see a different kind of magic, because
I knew the real man, and let me tell you, that man was a pistol.
Even though he didn't state his aphorism as he started out each day,
he may as well have, because that's the way he lived his life,
and it touched every person he came in contact with.

I know this, because it touched me as well, in a way I will never forget—and of all his laudable traits, it was truly the one I admire the most. So thank you, Pop, for showing me the magic, and for letting me share in your "magic time." It's a lesson well learned. And one I hope to pass on.

Chris Lemmon
ACTOR, WRITER, SON OF JACK LEMMON

The Key Advice
I Learned from My Dad

Don't make your days into a series of petty battles
and unpleasant moments—enjoy your life!

Charlie Matthau
DIRECTOR, SON OF WALTER MATTHAU

The Key to Laughter

Letting go.

Tim Allen
ACTOR, COMEDIAN

The Key to Tying the Knot

Having a girl who is willing to "hang in there."

Mickey Rooney
ACTOR, MARRIED TO HIS EIGHTH WIFE, JAN, FOR THIRTY YEARS

The Key to Originality

To paraphrase Emerson,
the understanding that we all lie in the lap
of an immense intelligence and our
originality is only as good as our receptors.

Norman Lear
TELEVISION WRITER, DIRECTOR, PRODUCER, ACTIVIST

The Key to Taking a Risk

I think of the key as a *willingness* to take risks.
What happened to me, I'd reached a point
where I was finally able to write novels
full time, with enough in the bank that
my family could get by for six months.
No more rising at five a.m. to write for
two hours before going to work at an ad agency.
But . . . we bought a house. The savings were
swallowed whole by the down payment and
I was back in advertising, now as a one-man
shop preparing ads for low-budget clients.

For two years I also wrote history and geography
scripts for Encyclopaedia Britannica Films,
all the while anxious to get back to writing fiction.
What I did I think of as "making my run."
I cut my workload in half to concentrate on
writing a novel, and made up for the loss of
income by delaying payments to suppliers
and magazines that ran my clients' ads.
I had to finish the book and sell it, or have to
re-mortgage the house that got me into this fix.

have more freedom for

rtunities for self-advance-

appiness than they have

he other, startled

of the American

not as human as any

the very class

The risk paid off.

The book even sold as a movie—not one that's memorable, but it got me out of advertising for good, allowing me to write books as a full-time occupation.

Elmore Leonard
AUTHOR AND SCREENWRITER

The Key to Believing

The key to believing that my brother Bob would recover was the incredible strength of the bond that my brothers and I have. The mutual support we provided each other and the support provided by the rest of our family members created a rock-solid structure that wouldn't allow my faith in his eventual recovery to fail.

Even in the earliest days of Bob's injury, I never allowed the idea that there could be just three brothers, or a somehow diminished person in Bob . . . it just wasn't an option.

When he woke up on March 6, 2006, after being in a coma, and it became apparent that he had emerged at a miraculous recovery level even at that early stage, my belief in his eventual complete recovery grew, bolstered again by the "bond of four brothers" we have been blessed with.

Dave Woodruff
BROTHER OF BROADCAST JOURNALIST BOB WOODRUFF

The Key to
Making Someone Smile

I don't have the key, but I'm constantly
looking for it. That's been my whole life.
I've dedicated every moment of my life
to the search for that key.

Howie Mandel
COMEDIAN AND ACTOR

The Key to
an Everlasting Love

Desire, friendship, hard work, honor,
laughter, and passion.
Opening your heart fully to
the blessed experience
of being one with another.

Billie Perry
WIFE OF JOE PERRY OF AEROSMITH,
CELEBRATING TWENTY-ONE YEARS OF MARRIAGE

The Key to an Everlasting Love

Once you have found your soulmate

(it may take a few tries),

don't ever take it for granted.

Unexpected flowers and romantic notes

are just as important twenty years down the road

as the first week you met!

Keep your heart and soul and ears open

so you can change and grow together

as your love blossoms.

Joe Perry
MUSICIAN AND SONGWRITER,
CELEBRATING TWENTY-ONE YEARS OF MARRIAGE

The Key to
Connecting to Animals

Love.

Doris Day
ACTRESS AND ANIMAL ACTIVIST

The Key to Staying Focused

With every goal, give it a hundred and fifty percent.
Never be dissuaded by rejection.
Remember, it is just one person's opinion,
and that person is wrong.

Linda Solomon
PHOTOJOURNALIST

·*Acknowledgments*·

I wish to thank the following key people for all of their guidance and time in making this book very special to me:

Jennifer Levesque, Leslie Stoker, Galen Smith, Anna Christian, Jennifer Gates, Amanda Murray, Joanna Shimkus-Poitier, Linda Dozoretz, Randall Tallerico, Ashley Atwater, Kelli Dade, Joan Walters (Micki), Teri Jones Tavour and Deb Goodman of Jones Photo, Tara Steinberg, Bryant Renfroe, Celia Borofsky, Teresa Hughes, Mimi McDowell, Jean-Pierre Trebot, Susan Duff, Frank Stella, Karen Ginsburg, Lana Morgan, Victoria Varela, Sylvia Weiner, Lauren Mitchell, Nancy Olmstead, Michelle Goldberg, Ralph Finch, Lori Weiss, Kevin Pawley, Doc Griffin, Amanda Bushey, Theresa Corigliano, Claire Cashin, Louise Riggio, Lisa Lapides Sawicki, and Mida Giragosian. Thanks also goes out to all of the amazing people who have contributed their words of wisdom for this book. Last, I cannot forget to acknowledge my Nikon FE-2 and Kodak Tri-X film!